HEROIC JOBS

FIGHTING CRIME

Ellen Labrecque

www.raintreepublishers.co.uk
Visit our website to find out
more information about
Raintree books.

To order:
☎ Phone 0845 6044371
🖷 Fax +44 (0) 1865 312263
🖳 Email myorders@raintreepublishers.co.uk

Customers from outside the UK please telephone +44 1865 312262

Raintree is an imprint of **Capstone Global Library Limited**,
a company incorporated in England and Wales having
its registered office at 7 Pilgrim Street, London, EC4V 6LB –
Registered company number: 6695582.

Text © Capstone Global Library Limited 2012
First published in hardback in 2012
Paperback edition first published in 2013

Edited by Dan Nunn, Rebecca Rissman, and Catherine
Veitch
Designed by Joanne Malivoire
Picture research by Elizabeth Alexander
Originated by Capstone Global Library
Printed and bound in China by CTPS

ISBN 978 1 406 23206 6 (hardback)
15 14 13 12 11
10 9 8 7 6 5 4 3 2 1

ISBN 978 1 406 23213 4 (paperback)
16 15 14 13 12
10 9 8 7 6 5 4 3 2 1

British Library Cataloguing in Publication Data
Labrecque, Ellen.
Fighting crime. – (Heroic jobs)
363.2-dc22
A full catalogue record for this book is available from the
British Library.

Acknowledgements
We would like to thank the following for permission
to reproduce photographs: © Newspix / News
Ltd / 3rd Party Managed Reproduction & Supply
Rights p. 20 (James Elsby); Alamy pp. 5 (© Les
Gibbon), 6 (© Les Gibbon), 11 (© David J. Green),
14 (© Altered Images), 17 (© Les Gibbon), 19
(© Jeff Greenberg), 22 (© Michael Matthews –
Police Images), 26 (© JHB Photography); Corbis
pp.18 (© Miguel Fernandes/epa), 21 (© Enrique
Marcarian/Reuters), 24 (© Ed Kashi), 25
(© Stephanie Sinclair/VII); Getty Images pp. 4
(Attila Kisbenedek/AFP), 7 (Metropolitan Police), 9
(Chris Jackson), 10 (FRANCOIS LO PRESTI/AFP), 12
(Nicholas Maeterlinck/AFP), 15 (EVARISTO SA/AFP),
16 (David Hartley/Bloomberg): iStockphoto p. 28
(© Terraxplorer); Photolibrary pp. 8 (Jochen Tack),
13 (moodboard), 27 (Alain Le Bot/Photononstop);
Rex Features pp. 23 (Nils Jorgensen),
29 Daniel Graves.

Cover photograph of police cars in action reproduced with
permission of Photolibrary (Jochen Tack/Imagebroker.net).

Every effort has been made to contact copyright holders
of material reproduced in this book. Any omissions will be
rectified in subsequent printings if notice is given to the
publisher.

We would like to thank Mark Oddi for his invaluable help in
the preparation of this book.

Some words are shown in bold, **like this**. You can find
out what they mean by looking in the glossary.

Contents

Action!

The time is 5:00 a.m. Most people are asleep, except police officers on a raid. The officers surround the house of a suspected criminal. They rap loudly on the door and shout to be let in. When nobody answers, the officers break the door down and charge in.

What is a police raid?

A police raid is when police officers surprise **suspects** and **arrest** them, or search for **evidence**. Suspects are people that the police think are guilty of a crime. Raids are used when police think the suspects will **resist**, or fight against, the arrest.

Did you know?
Police raids that take place in the early morning are also called "dawn raids".

Who are the police?

Police officers are in charge of keeping order in their local area. Officers stop, or **prevent**, crime from happening. They also discover, or **detect**, crime. They must be smart and honest. They must also be very fit.

8

Police officers also need to be brave.

Police **investigate**, or research facts about a crime, before making a raid. During an investigation, police officers collect **evidence** to prove what has happened. They also **interrogate** people who may have seen what happened. These people are called **witnesses**.

Teamwork works

Each member of the police raid team has a job. Some officers look for **evidence** at the scene of the crime. Other officers are **lookouts**. Lookouts watch to make sure the **suspect** doesn't escape. They also keep people away from the crime scene.

Dogs are part of the team, too.

Raids can be dangerous. Police never know for certain what they will find. There could be more **suspects** than they first thought. There could also be explosives, such as bombs, or loaded guns. The more prepared the police are, the safer they will be.

All these weapons were seized in a police raid in November 2010, in Rio de Janeiro, Brazil.

Equipment

Each police officer wears about 16 kilograms of equipment on a raid. The equipment includes a bulletproof or a stab vest to protect against getting hurt, a radio, and handcuffs to **arrest** the **suspects**.

radio

stab vest

POLICE

Did you know?

A police officer may use a taser gun to fire an electric shock at a suspect if the suspect is threatning them with violence. Usually, a taser gun does no long-term harm.

17

Some police raids are to recover stolen goods. In a raid near Sydney, Australia, in January 2009, police discovered the country's biggest shoplifting crime ever. A large warehouse was filled with stolen make-up, perfumes, razor blades, and shampoos. The total value of the **loot** was millions of pounds.

Did you know? Some stolen paintings can be worth millions of pounds.

Escape!

Sometimes, a suspected criminal escapes in a car during a police raid. The police drive after the suspect. Police helicopters also fly above the cars. They tell the officers in the police car which way the **suspect** is driving.

23

Sometimes, the police will get some secret information, or a **tip-off**, to tell them that a crime is going to take place. They set up **surveillance**, or keep watch, at the place where the suspected crime is supposed to happen. Then, they can catch the criminals red-handed!

25

Becoming a police officer

You need to be brave to become a police officer. You will need to train at a police training centre, as well as pass written and spoken tests. Police officers should be smart and fit. They are the world's real superheroes. They are crime fighters!

26

27

Stay safe

In an emergency, call for help. It is important to give as much information about the emergency as possible. Never ever make **hoax** 999 calls. It could cost lives. When someone has phoned 999, the emergency services will soon be at the scene.

Did you know?
There are different emergency telephone numbers around the world:
- Australia: 000
- most of Europe: 112
- UK: 999
- United States: 911

Glossary

arrest catch someone and charge them with a crime

detect discover or catch

evidence something found that can prove or disprove that a crime took place

hoax trick, where someone says something has happened, but they are not telling the truth

illegally do something that is against the law

interrogate ask questions in a serious manner

investigate try to find out the truth about something

lookout person who watches for danger

loot stolen goods or money

prevent stop from happening

resist try to stop something from happening

surveillance watch kept over a person

suspect someone who is thought to have done something wrong

tip-off piece of private or secret information

witness somone who sees an event, such as a crime, happening and can tell other people about it

Find out more

Books

A Career as a Police Officer, Stephanie Watson
(Rosen Classroom, 2010)

Call the Police, Cath Senker (Franklin Watts, 2010)

Emergency 999 Police, Kathryn Walker
(Wayland Publishers, 2011)

Websites

www.billtheburglar.org/
This website has tips on ways to secure your home
against burglars.

www.police.uk/?view=force_sites
A list with links to all the sites of police forces
around the United Kingdom.

**www.police.vic.gov.au/content.asp?Document_
ID=12260**
This website about a police force in Australia is
packed with interesting facts about the police
and fun activities.

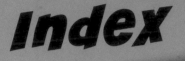

Index